Simplysoups

for summer and winter

Editorial director: Brigitte Éveno

Design and layout: Guylaine & Christophe Moi

Production: Caroline Artémon

Editorial assistant: Sylvie Gauthier

Translation by Laura Washburn for JMS Books LLP

Design US edition Chris Bell

The editors would like to thank Maïté Lapierre for her invaluable assistance

© Hachette 2001
This edition © Hachette Livre (Hachette Pratique) 2003
This edition published by Hachette Illustrated UK, Octopus Publishing Group,
2–4 Heron Quays, London E14 4JP
English translation by JMS Books LLP (email: moseleystrachan@blueyonder.co.uk)
Translation © Octopus Publishing Group

A CIP catalogue for this book is available from the British Library

ISBN: 1 84430 039 0

Printed by Tien Wah, Singapore

Simply soups
for summer and winter

Sophie Brissaud

Photographs by Jean-Blaise Hall
Styling by Valérie Lhomme

HACHETTE
Illustrated

acknowledgments

Valérie Lhomme would like to thank
the following suppliers who kindly lent
props: Quartz, La Forge Subtile, Monastica
and Blanc d'Ivoire. She would also like to
thank Alice, Tristan, Victor, and Philippe,
who accepted the invitation to come along
one Wednesday and sample some of the
soups under the skillful eye of Jean-Blaise
Hall's camera.

contents

summer soups

introduction

The weather's fine and a warm breeze is blowing. Perhaps the leaves are gently rustling, or there's a distant sound of waves crashing on the shore. It's a time to be lazy, but that's no reason to stop entertaining. And a chilled soup is the perfect way to begin a relaxing meal with friends. These soups are easily made in advance and kept in the refrigerator until serving, adding a touch of refined elegance to a balmy summer feast.

Chilled soups are not a new invention: they have been around for ages, and we are only just rediscovering them. They have long been popular in southern and eastern European countries, where these refreshing delicacies are savored slowly, to combat the stifling heat. What a delicious way to cool down, with a cold consommé, a creamy chilled soup, or a sparkling jelled treat. Warm soups also contribute to a summer menu. These are lighter and more invigorating than their cold-weather counterparts, filled with sun-gorged ingredients and more adventurous flavors, such as fruit or sweet-and-sour. For the most part, warm summer soups work just as well served chilled; however, the reverse is not always possible, since cold soups often rely on uncooked ingredients for their character.

Cream of cucumber with mint

• Bring 1 cup of water to a boil in a small saucepan. Add the bouillon cube and stir to dissolve. Set aside to cool.

• Wash and shred the mint sprigs. Wash the cucumbers and peel in stripes, leaving some skin intact. Cut in half lengthwise and scoop out the seeds. Slice the cucumber halves.

• In a food processor or blender, purée the cucumber slices with the mint, dill, chicken bouillon, whipping cream, and sugar, working in batches if necessary. Transfer to a large bowl and mix well. Season with pepper, cover, and refrigerate for at least 2 hours.

• To serve, taste for seasoning, then ladle into chilled bowls, adding a dollop of crème fraîche to each one. Garnish with extra cucumber slices and chives.

Serves 4–6
Preparation: 30 minutes
Refrigeration: at least
2 hours

1 chicken bouillon cube
7–8 sprigs of fresh mint
2 firm hothouse cucumbers
3 sprigs of fresh dill weed
1 cup whipping cream
1 tablespoon sugar
salt and freshly ground white pepper
6 tablespoons crème fraîche
a few fresh chives and extra cucumber slices, for garnish

Jelled beet consommé

• Peel and rinse the beets, then cut into cubes. Put in a saucepan together with 2 cups of water and bring to a boil, then lower the heat, cover, and simmer gently for 40 minutes. Drain, reserving the cooking liquid, and set to one side.

• Add the stock, vinegar, celery seeds, and dried dill to the beet cooking liquid. Bring to a boil, then lower the heat and simmer for 10 minutes. Taste for seasoning.

Serves 4
Preparation: 25 minutes
Cooking time: 35 minutes
Refrigeration: 6 hours

2 raw beets
2 cups vegetable or beef stock
1 tablespoon red wine vinegar
pinch of celery seeds
pinch of dried dill weed
6 gelatin sheets
4 tablespoons thick, plain yogurt
1 bunch of fresh chives
1 lemon
salt and freshly ground white pepper

• Strain the broth through a coffee filter. Season with pepper. Add the gelatin sheets and stir gently until melted. Add the beet cubes. Cover and refrigerate until mixture is thick and syrupy. Stir well, then cover again and refrigerate until set.

• To serve, break up the jelled mixture with a spoon and divide among serving bowls. Top each with a dollop of yogurt, snipped chives, and slices of lemon.

Vichyssoise with watercress

• Peel the potatoes and cut into cubes. Peel the garlic. Choose a few leafy watercress sprigs and set aside; chop the rest, without untying the bunch, close to the stems. Wash and dry thoroughly.

• In a large saucepan, combine two-thirds of the chopped watercress, the potatoes, garlic, and stock. Bring to a boil, then lower the heat, cover, and simmer gently for 20 minutes. Purée in a food processor or blender, then return to the pan. Stir in the whipping cream and season. Bring just to simmering point, then remove from the heat. Taste for seasoning, cover, and set aside.

Serves 4–6
Preparation: 30 minutes
Cooking time: 20 minutes
Refrigeration: 2 hours

4–5 new potatoes
1 garlic clove
2 bunches of watercress
3 cups chicken stock
1¼ cups whipping cream
4 tablespoons crème fraîche
salt and freshly ground white pepper

• Combine most of the reserved watercress leaves and the crème fraîche in a small food processor or blender, and purée. Stir the delicate green cream into the soup, cover, and let cool until lukewarm. Refrigerate for at least 2 hours.

• To serve, taste for seasoning, then ladle into bowls and decorate each with a swirl of whipping cream and a few watercress sprigs.

Creamy Mexican zucchini soup

Serves 4
Preparation:
30 minutes
Cooking time:
40 minutes
Refrigeration:
at least 6 hours

4 young, firm zucchini

2 tablespoons chopped fresh cilantro

1 small onion

2 tablespoons clarified butter

1 tablespoon flour

1 cup evaporated milk or whipping cream

1 cup chicken stock

salt and freshly ground pepper

sprigs of fresh cilantro and zucchini flowers, for garnish (optional)

• Wash the zucchini, then cut into large pieces. Put them in a saucepan with enough cold water to cover. Bring to a boil, then cover and simmer gently for 20 minutes. Remove from the heat and let cool, uncovered, until lukewarm.

• In a food processor, combine the zucchini, 1 cup of their cooking liquid, and the chopped cilantro. Process until smooth.

• Peel and mince the onion. Heat the butter in a saucepan, add the onion, and cook over low heat until soft, about 15 minutes. Add the flour and stir well, then add the zucchini purée, the evaporated milk or cream, and the stock. Whisk gently to combine. Season and bring to a gentle simmer: do not allow to boil.

• Remove from the heat and let cool, then refrigerate for at least 6 hours. To serve, garnish with cilantro sprigs and zucchini flowers, if available.

• This soup can also be served hot.

Serves 6
Preparation: 40 minutes
Cooking time: 1 hour 40 minutes
Soaking time: 12 hours

$1/2$ cup small, dried white beans • $1/2$ teaspoon baking soda • 1 onion • 6 large garlic cloves, inner green shoots removed • 2 turnips • 2 carrots • 1 small celery stalk • 3 ripe tomatoes • 1 cup olive oil • 1 fresh bouquet garni (thyme, bay leaf, savory) • 1 small slice of pumpkin or other winter squash • 2 small zucchini • handful of fine green beans • 2 leeks, white part only • 1 small bunch of fresh flat-leaf parsley • 1 large bunch of fresh basil, with large leaves • $1/3$ cup pine nuts • $1/2$ cup grated Parmesan cheese (or use pecorino) • large handful (or more if desired) of small pasta shapes, such as macaroni • salt and freshly ground pepper

Provençal vegetable soup (soupe au pistou)

• Soak the beans overnight in enough cold water to cover, with the baking soda. The following day, drain, put them in a pan, cover with fresh water, and cook until tender, 30–40 minutes. Drain.

• Chop the onion, 2 of the garlic cloves, the turnips, carrots, and celery into small cubes. Peel, seed, and chop the tomatoes.

• Heat some of the olive oil in a large saucepan. Add the onion, garlic, carrots, celery, turnips, and drained beans, and cook gently for a few minutes. Add the tomatoes and cover with plenty of cold water. Bring to a boil and season lightly. Add the bouquet garni, lower the heat, cover, and simmer gently for 40 minutes.

• Meanwhile, cube the peeled pumpkin and zucchini, and slice the green beans into short pieces. Slice the leek whites and chop the parsley. Wash and dry the basil.

• To make the pistou, peel the remaining garlic cloves. Put into a mortar and pestle with the pine nuts, basil, and Parmesan, and crush. Gradually add the remaining olive oil to obtain a thick paste. Set aside.

• Add the leeks, pumpkin, zucchini, green beans, pasta, and parsley to the soup. Taste for seasoning and add more water if necessary. Simmer gently for 15 minutes. Just before serving, stir in the pistou.

Variation: In Provence, France, 2 ripe tomatoes, peeled, seeded, and chopped, are sometimes added to the pistou.

Chilled arugula soup

• Wash and dry the arugula; remove any stems. Take one handful and mince it, then set aside.

• Coarsely chop the white part of the green onions. Heat the olive oil in a saucepan, add the chopped onions, and cook for 2 minutes. Add the whole arugula leaves and half the stock. Bring to a boil, then lower the heat and simmer gently for 1–2 minutes, until the arugula just begins to wilt. Transfer to a food processor or blender and purée. Return to the pan, add the remaining stock, and simmer gently for 2 minutes; do not allow to boil. Remove from the heat and stir in the cream and minced arugula. Season with salt and pepper. Cover and refrigerate for at least 2 hours.

• Hard-cook the eggs. Peel under cold, running water and let cool. Chop the yolks and one of the whites (discard the other). Snip the chives and mix with the chopped egg. Salt lightly and set aside.

• To serve, ladle the soup into bowls or tall glasses and garnish with the egg and chive mixture and thyme flowers.

Serves 4
Preparation: 40 minutes
Cooking time: 4 minutes
Refrigeration time: at least 2 hours

10 oz fresh arugula
4 green onions
2 tablespoons olive oil
3 cups chicken stock
1 cup whipping cream
2 eggs
a few fresh chives
salt and freshly ground pepper
a few fresh thyme flowers, for garnish

Strawberry soup with balsamic vinegar

• Lightly rinse the strawberries and remove the hulls. Choose 20 of the best ones, cut them in half, and sprinkle with half the sugar and 2 tablespoons of the balsamic vinegar. Refrigerate for 2 hours.

• Combine the remaining strawberries, sugar, and vinegar with the orange and lemon zests and Grand Marnier or orange juice in a food processor, and purée. Transfer to a large bowl and stir well until the sugar is completely dissolved. Whisk in the yogurt. Refrigerate for 2 hours.

• Serve in shallow bowls, garnished with the marinated strawberry halves and a few drizzles of the marinade.

• This dish makes a delicious appetizer, and can also be served as a dessert.

Serves 4-6
Preparation:
20 minutes
Marinating time:
at least 2 hours

2 lb ripe, sweet strawberries (or use Alpine strawberries)

1 cup sugar

6 tablespoons balsamic vinegar from Modena

$^1/_2$ teaspoon finely grated orange zest

$^1/_2$ teaspoon finely grated lemon zest

1 tablespoon Grand Marnier (or use orange juice)

2 cups thick, plain yogurt

Helpful hints for summer

For most of these recipes, you will need good stock. Here are some guidelines for preparing simple, basic stocks and enhancing them according to taste and available ingredients.

• **Vegetable stock:** carrots, turnips, leeks, onions, garlic, celery or celeriac, herbs, and black peppercorns can all be combined; you could also add parsnips, tomatoes, fennel, beets (which will give you a deep red stock), cabbage, etc. Cover the vegetables and herbs with plenty of cold water, salt lightly, and bring to a boil. Lower the heat and simmer gently for 1½ hours. Strain.

• **Fish stock:** use the bones and heads from white fish (flatfish such as sole or flounder are ideal) and add carrots, onions, shallots, leek whites, herbs, black peppercorns, a splash of white wine, and some fennel seeds. Bring to a boil, then add salt and simmer gently for 30 minutes. Strain well before using.

• Delicately flavored ingredients have different stock requirements: do not use strong stocks that would overpower them (in a cold soup, however, a stronger stock may be needed for a fuller flavor). When using water, be sure to use filtered or spring water whenever possible.

• Locally grown produce is more readily available in summer than in winter, so take advantage of the seasonal glut. Buy everything as fresh as possible, and use quickly for optimum flavor and nutritional value. In an ideal world, keep fresh produce out of the refrigerator: The cold hardens green peas, makes asparagus woody, spoils mushrooms, and strips strawberries of their flavor. So cook as soon as possible after purchase. Take care to let chilled soups cool to room temperature before refrigerating.

Normandy apple and potato soup

- Slice the leeks. Peel the tart apples and the potatoes, and cut into cubes.
- Heat 4 tablespoons of the butter in a large saucepan, add the leeks, and cook to soften, about 3 minutes. Add the apple cubes and cook for 5 more minutes, stirring often, then add the potatoes and stock. Bring to a boil, then lower the heat, cover, and simmer gently for 40 minutes.
- Transfer to a food processor or blender and purée. Stir in the cream and cinnamon. Season with salt and pepper, then cover and refrigerate for at least 2 hours.
- Peel and slice the firm-fleshed apples. Cook in the remaining butter until golden, about 5 minutes, stirring often.
- Serve the soup in bowls, garnished with the apple slices and a dash of Calvados, if using.
- This soup can also be served hot.

Serves 4–6
Preparation: 30 minutes
Cooking time: 40 minutes
Refrigeration: at least 2 hours

2 leeks, white part only

2 lb tart apples, such as Granny Smith or pippin

2 new potatoes

6 tablespoons clarified butter

6 cups chicken stock

1 cup whipping cream

pinch of ground cinnamon

2 firm-fleshed apples, such as York Imperial

salt and freshly ground white pepper

Calvados, for serving (optional)

Andalucian hake soup

- Cut the fish into slices about 3 inches thick. Salt generously and let stand for 1 hour.
- Peel the garlic. Trim the crust from the bread and cut into cubes. Cook the bread cubes in ½ cup of the olive oil until golden and crisp, then rub with 2 of the garlic cloves. Set aside and keep warm.
- Heat the remaining oil in a large saucepan and gently fry the remaining whole garlic cloves. As soon as they begin to turn golden, add the onion and cook over low heat for 1 more minute. Do not let the onion brown. Add 6 cups of boiling water, then cover and simmer gently for 20 minutes. Raise the heat and add the fish pieces, one at a time, maintaining a constant boil. Cook for 15 minutes over medium heat. You can cook the fish for a shorter time, but the broth will have less flavor.
- Just before serving, stir in the orange juice. Serve in a heated terracotta tureen, with the croutons. Aïoli (garlic mayonnaise) goes well with this dish, though it is not traditional.

Serves 4-6
Preparation: 20 minutes
Cooking time: 35 minutes
Standing time: 1 hour

**2 lb whole hake or whiting
(1 or 2, depending on size),
gutted and scaled**

10 large garlic cloves

**6 slices of rustic sourdough bread,
such as Poilâne**

1¼ cups olive oil

1 large onion, minced

**⅔ cup bitter Seville orange juice
(or use the juice of 1 lime and
1 clementine)**

Aïoli (optional, see page 34)

salt

Serves 4-6
Preparation: 30 minutes
Cooking time: 20 minutes
Refrigeration: 6 hours

6 cups chicken stock • pinch of ground allspice • small pinch of cayenne
• 3 tablespoons long-grain rice • 4 extra large fresh eggs • juice of 3 lemons
• 6 lemon slices • grated nutmeg • salt and freshly ground white pepper

Greek egg and lemon soup

• Put the stock in a large saucepan with the allspice and cayenne. Bring to a boil, then add the rice. Lower the heat and cook for 15 minutes; the rice should be tender on the outside but still slightly firm to the bite. Turn the heat down as low as possible.

• Beat the eggs vigorously, as if making an omelette. Gradually whisk in the lemon juice; the mixture will lighten in color. Add a ladleful of the simmering stock to the egg mixture, whisking constantly. Add another ladleful and then a third, still whisking. Pour the egg and stock mixture into the pan. Return the soup just to a simmer, stirring gently; do not let it boil. As soon as the soup thickens, remove from the heat. Taste for seasoning.

• Cover and let cool. Refrigerate for at least 6 hours. Serve chilled, garnished with lemon slices and a sprinkling of freshly grated nutmeg.

Variation: For a smooth, creamy consistency, purée the soup in a blender after adding the egg and lemon mixture.

Hungarian chicken and grape soup

Serves 6–8
Preparation: 1 hour
Cooking time about 2 hours

36 large, white grapes • 1 small head celeriac • 3 carrots • 1 small onion • 1 parsnip • 1 free-range chicken, about 2 lb • 1 fresh bouquet garni (4 sprigs of flat-leaf parsley, 1 leafy end of a celery stalk, 1 sprig of thyme) • 1 cup sweet white wine, such as Jurançon, Loupiac, or Monbazillac • 2 lemons, halved • 3 sugar cubes • 1 tablespoon chicken or duck fat • 2 tablespoons flour • 4 tablespoons crème fraîche • salt and freshly ground white pepper

• Peel and seed the grapes; cover and set aside. Peel all the vegetables and cut into fine dice.

• Put the chicken into a large saucepan and add 10 cups of water and some salt. Bring to a simmer, then add a splash of cold water to prevent boiling. Skim, then repeat this process three times. Add the bouquet garni and the vegetables. Cook over low heat until the chicken is tender, about 1½ hours.

• Remove the bouquet garni. Take out the chicken; dice all the meat and set aside. Strain the stock and set aside, keeping several carrot cubes for garnish. Put the wine in a saucepan, add the lemons and sugar, and bring to a boil. Boil for 10 minutes. Remove the lemons and squeeze all their juice into the wine; discard the lemon halves. Add the grapes to the warm wine, cover, and let steep for 5 minutes.

• Heat the poultry fat in a small pan and add the flour. Cook gently until the mixture just begins to turn golden. Add a few spoonfuls of stock and stir well, then pour this roux into the reserved stock, stirring well. Add the diced chicken and simmer for 5 minutes.

• Before serving, stir in the wine and grape mixture and the crème fraîche. Taste for seasoning. Serve garnished with carrot cubes.

Serves 4–6
Preparation: 45 minutes
Refrigeration: about 2 hours

4 slices of white bread, crusts removed • 7 oz large, white grapes (about 2 cups) • 2 large garlic cloves • 1$^1/_3$ cups blanched almonds • 1–2 tablespoons red wine vinegar • $^3/_4$ cup extra virgin olive oil • handful of slivered almonds • salt and freshly ground pepper

Almond gazpacho

• Break up the bread slices and reduce to fine crumbs in a food processor. Let soak in water for 30 minutes. Peel the grapes, cut in half, and remove the seeds. Put in a bowl, cover, and set aside. Squeeze the bread crumbs dry with your hands. Peel the garlic and remove any green sprouts from the center.

• Combine the bread crumbs, garlic, blanched almonds, vinegar, and oil in a food processor. Process until smooth. Transfer to a serving bowl and refrigerate for 2 hours.

• Before serving, dilute with water to the desired consistency. Season with salt and pepper, and add the grapes. Garnish with the slivered almonds and serve, with chilled white wine.

Hungarian sour cherry soup

• Pit the cherries and set aside. Put the cherry pits in a saucepan with enough water to cover. Bring to a boil, then lower the heat and simmer gently for 30 minutes. Strain and measure the liquid. You will need 6 cups , so add water as necessary to make this quantity. Set aside.

• In a bowl, stir together the crème fraîche, flour, salt, and confectioners' sugar to obtain a thick paste. Set aside.

• Put the cherries in a saucepan and add the measured cooking liquid and the granulated sugar. Bring to a boil, then lower the heat and simmer for 20 minutes. Transfer 2 ladlefuls of the cherry liquid to the crème fraîche paste and whisk for 2 minutes, then pour this crème fraîche mixture into the soup, stirring well. Add the cinnamon, if using. Simmer, uncovered, for 5 minutes, then remove from the heat, cover, and let cool. Taste for seasoning; you should be able to detect a slight salty taste.

• This is a traditional Hungarian recipe, always served chilled, and always as an appetizer. The cherry pits add a seductive bitterness, but they can be omitted.

Serves 6
Preparation: 50 minutes
Cooking time: 55 minutes

1 lb sour cherries (about 5 cups)
1 cup crème fraîche
2 tablespoons flour
1 teaspoon confectioners' sugar
1 cup granulated sugar
2 pinches of ground cinnamon
(optional)
pinch of salt

French fish soup (bourride)

• Cut the fish into thick slices. Season lightly and squeeze over some lemon juice. Set aside.

• Peel the potatoes and cook in boiling salted water until tender. Set aside in their cooking liquid to keep warm.

• Put the fish stock into a large saucepan and add half the leeks, a slice of lemon, the thyme, parsley stems, bay leaf, and vinegar. Bring to a boil, then simmer gently for 25 minutes. Strain and set aside.

• To make the aïoli, peel the garlic cloves and remove any green sprouts from the center. Mix with the bread crumbs and crush in a mortar and pestle (or a food processor). Season with salt and pepper, add the egg yolks, and mix well. Gradually mix in olive oil, pouring slowly, until you have a mayonnaise-like texture. Add the lemon juice. Transfer to a large bowl and set aside.

• Heat some olive oil in a large pan. Add the remaining chopped leeks and the crushed garlic. Put the fish pieces on top and add the stock. Bring slowly to a boil, then simmer gently for 10 minutes.

• Remove the fish pieces and put in a large soup tureen with the drained potatoes; keep warm. Reduce the fish stock by one-third. Stir in the crème fraîche and remove from the heat. Gradually incorporate the fish stock into the aïoli, a little at a time, whisking constantly. The soup should thicken. Pour over the fish and serve immediately, garnished with chopped parsley leaves.

Serves 6
Preparation: 1½ hours
Cooking time: 35 minutes

2 lb boneless monkfish tail
(or use halibut fillet)
1–2 lemons
1½ lb new potatoes
6 cups fish stock
2 leeks, white part only
1 sprig of fresh thyme
1 bunch of fresh flat-leaf parsley
1 bay leaf
1 tablespoon wine vinegar
1 garlic clove, crushed
2 tablespoons crème fraîche
salt and freshly ground pepper

• **For the aïoli:**
4 garlic cloves
1 tablespoon fine, fresh bread crumbs
2–3 egg yolks
extra virgin olive oil
juice of ½ lemon

Senegalese shrimp soup with coconut

• Heat the butter in a heavy pan and add the onion. Cook over low heat until soft, about 10 minutes. Add the curry powder and flour, and cook for 5 more minutes, stirring constantly. Add the coconut milk, then the stock, whisking until there are no more lumps. Simmer gently for 10 minutes, stirring occasionally.

• Whisk the egg yolks in a bowl. Remove the soup from the heat and add it to the yolks, little by little, whisking until fully incorporated. Return the mixture to the pan, set over low heat, and add the chicken and shrimp. Cook until warmed through; do not allow to boil. Remove from the heat and taste for seasoning. Let cool, then refrigerate for at least 2 hours.

• Before serving, stir in the whipping cream. Serve well chilled, accompanied by cubes of pear and banana for garnish.

• This soup, which has Anglo-Indian origins, is very rich, so serve in small quantities.

Serves 4-6
Preparation: 25 minutes
Cooking time: 20 minutes
Refrigeration: at least
2 hours

2 tablespoons clarified butter
1 onion, minced
2 teaspoons best quality curry powder
1 tablespoon flour
1 cup coconut milk
3$\frac{1}{3}$ cups strong chicken stock
2 egg yolks
1 cup diced cooked chicken breast
1 cup roughly chopped peeled, cooked shrimp
2 cups whipping cream, chilled
1 firm, ripe pear
1 banana
salt and freshly ground pepper

Indian tomato soup

Serves 4
Preparation:
35 minutes
Cooking time:
20 minutes

9 large garlic cloves

3 tablespoons clarified butter or olive oil

pinch of coarsely ground pepper

6 whole cloves

1 bay leaf

large pinch of asafetida (available from Indian markets)

14 oz canned peeled tomatoes

1 teaspoon turmeric

1 teaspoon ground fenugreek

1/2 teaspoon ground cumin

pinch of cayenne

2 sprigs of fresh curry leaves

1 tablespoon lime juice

1 chicken bouillon cube (or 1 cup strong chicken stock)

• **For the garnish:**

1/2 teaspoon cumin seeds

1 teaspoon black mustard seeds

1 teaspoon crushed urad dal (small white lentils)

3 tablespoons chopped fresh cilantro

• Peel the garlic. Heat 1 tablespoon of the butter or oil and add 8 of the garlic cloves. Cook gently until golden all over. As soon as they begin to color, add the coarsely ground pepper, cloves, and bay leaf. When they are well colored, add the asafetida, tomatoes, all the ground spices, the curry leaves, lime juice, bouillon cube, and 1 cup water (unless you are using stock). Bring to a boil, then cover, lower the heat, and simmer gently for 20 minutes. Remove and discard the bay leaf, curry leaves, and cloves, then work the soup through a fine sieve. Return to the pan, cover, and put over low heat to keep warm.

• To prepare the garnish, slice the remaining garlic clove. Heat the rest of the butter or oil and add the garlic slices, cumin and mustard seeds, and lentils. Cook over medium heat until golden. When the mustard seeds begin to pop, tip the mixture immediately into the soup. Stir well and add the cilantro. Cover and let stand, off the heat, for 3 minutes before serving.

• This soup can also be served cold, but not chilled.

Serves 6-8
Preparation: 25 minutes
Cooking time: 1 hour 20 minutes
Refrigeration: at least 2 hours

6 large, ripe pears, preferably Comice • 2 onions • 2 garlic cloves • ¼ cup clarified butter • 1 cup dry white wine • 6 cups chicken stock • 8 oz blue cheese, preferably Fourme d'Ambert, rind removed • 2 cups whipping cream • squeeze of lemon juice (optional) • 1 bunch of fresh chives • salt and freshly ground white pepper

Creamy pear soup with blue cheese

• Peel and core the pears and cut into cubes. Peel and mince the onions and garlic. Heat the butter in a large saucepan. Add the onions and garlic, and cook gently for 3 minutes. Add the pears and sweat for 10 minutes over medium heat. Deglaze the pan with the wine, stirring, and add the chicken stock. Bring to a boil, then lower the heat, cover and simmer gently for 1 hour.

• Crumble or crush the cheese with a fork.

Add to the soup and stir until completely melted. Purée the soup in a blender, then stir in the whipping cream. Season with salt and pepper, and add the lemon juice if desired. Let cool, then refrigerate for at least 2 hours.

• Serve chilled, garnished with snipped chives.

• You can replace the Fourme d'Ambert with any other blue cheese, such as Stilton or Roquefort.

Brazilian sweet potato soup

• Peel and mince the onion. Peel, seed, and chop the tomatoes. Peel the sweet potatoes, then cut into slices and put them in a heavy pan with the stock. Bring to a boil. Lower the heat, cover, and simmer gently for 20 minutes. Drain, reserving the stock.

• Heat the butter in a saucepan, add the onion, and cook over low heat until soft. Add the tomatoes and cook gently for 5 more minutes. Purée in a blender or food processor along with the sweet potatoes. Thin with some of the stock, if necessary. Return to the pan with the remaining stock. Season and reheat gently.

• Serve hot, garnished with chopped fresh cilantro if desired, although this soup is delicious just as it is.

Serves 6
Preparation: 25 minutes
Cooking time: 35 minutes

1 onion
4 ripe tomatoes (or use canned)
1 lb sweet potatoes, preferably with pale yellow flesh
4 cups beef stock
4 tablespoons unsalted butter
1 small bunch of fresh cilantro (optional)
salt and freshly ground pepper

Mango and melon soup

• Wash and shred the mint leaves, reserving a few whole ones for garnish. Peel the mangoes and cut the flesh from the central seed, working over a large bowl to catch all the juice. Peel the melon, remove seeds, and cut into cubes.

• In a food processor, combine the mango, melon, mint, lemon juice, confectioners' sugar, wine, and yogurt, and process until smooth. Transfer to a bowl and refrigerate for 2 hours.

• Pour into glass bowls and garnish with mint leaves. Serve well chilled, as an appetizer.

Serves 4-6
Preparation: 20 minutes
Refrigeration: at least
2 hours

2 sprigs of fresh mint
2 ripe mangoes
1 ripe cantaloupe melon
2 tablespoons lemon juice
1 tablespoon confectioners' sugar
$^2/_3$ cup dry white wine
2 tablespoons thick, plain yogurt

Ivory Coast avocado soup

• Scrub the lime well and cut in half. Squeeze the juice from one half; cut the other half into wafer-thin slices. Wearing rubber gloves to protect your hands, cut the chili pepper into quarters, and remove core and seeds. Mince one-quarter to one-half (according to taste); slice the remaining chili pepper thinly. Set aside.

• Cut the avocados in half and remove the pits. Scoop out the flesh with a spoon and put into a food processor. Blend until smooth. Gradually add the stock, processing between additions. Add the lime juice, yogurt, minced chili pepper, and a few grindings of pepper. Stir well, then cover and refrigerate for at least 1 hour.

• Before serving, taste for seasoning. Transfer to bowls and garnish with slices of lime and chili pepper.

Serves 4
Preparation: 30 minutes
Refrigeration: at least
1 hour

1 lime, with bright shiny skin
1 small, red, yellow, or orange hot chili pepper, such as Scotch Bonnet or habanero
2 large, ripe Haas avocados
4 cups cold chicken stock
1 tablespoon thick, plain yogurt
salt and freshly ground black pepper

Note: If you (or your guests) find this soup too hot, instead of using minced chili peppers, soak a few chili slices in the lime juice for 30 minutes. Remove the chili slices and use the juice as instructed in the recipe. This will give you the chili flavor with less of the fire.

winter soups

Recipe list

introduction

Soup is one of the first "real" foods most of us encounter, when we graduate from the bottle in babyhood. "Soup of the evening, beautiful soup"—the word conjures up notions of something soothing and nourishing, something that makes us grow big and strong. Later, when we are grown (because we ate our soup!), we discover the whole range of soups, with a universe of taste sensations. We learn of broths that are warming and soups that are comforting, served piping hot in warm bowls, with trails of aromatic steam. The world outside may be dreary, but inside it is warm and comforting. Eaten alone or in company, each spoonful of soup contains a discovery: a small cube of carrot, a slice of mushroom, a tiny piece of pasta, the pearly sheen of seafood in cream, a salty morsel of bacon, a thread of melted cheese. All the flavors mingle gloriously in soupy warmth; we can even make sensual additions such as truffles or porcini. Steaming hot bowls of soup in winter are a blessing to share with good company, when the storms rage outside and the bustle of the day has subsided. Soup is generally eaten in silence, for it demands peaceful contemplation.

Fish soup, Hamburg-style

• Sprinkle the eel pieces with salt and pepper, then let stand for 2 hours.

• Peel the pears and cut into thin slices. Bring the wine to a boil, add the pear slices and lemon peel, and poach until tender. Cover and set aside. In another pan, bring the beef stock to a boil, add the bouquet garni and cauliflower, and simmer gently for 15 minutes. Drain the cauliflower, reserving the stock.

• Put the eel in another saucepan and just cover with cold water. Add the bay leaf, onion, vinegar, and salt. Bring to a boil, then simmer gently for 15 minutes. Remove the fish and carefully extract all the bones. Put the boned eel in a soup tureen, with the pears and cauliflower, and keep warm in a low oven.

• Mix together the eel cooking liquid, the reserved beef stock, and the pear cooking liquid. Bring to a boil, then add the peas and simmer gently for 10–15 minutes. Taste for seasoning. Discard the bouquet garni and lemon peel.

• Mix the egg yolk with a few spoonfuls of hot broth, then pour back into the simmering pea mixture. Stir well and pour over the eel.

• Serve hot, accompanied by a wine from Alsace.

Note: The eel skin contributes a great deal of flavor, so do not remove it during cooking.

Serves 6
Preparation: 40 minutes
Cooking time: about
45 minutes
Standing time: 2 hours

1 lb eel, sliced (or use tuna, swordfish, or monkfish)

3 firm, ripe pears

²/₃ cup dry white wine

2-inch piece of lemon peel

6 cups beef stock

1 fresh bouquet garni (a couple of sprigs each of thyme, tarragon, and sage)

10 oz small cauliflower florets (about 3 cups)

1 bay leaf

1 onion, peeled, quartered, and sliced

splash of wine vinegar

1¹/₂ cups shelled fresh green peas

1 egg yolk

salt and freshly ground pepper

Cream of Jerusalem artichokes with caramelized mushrooms

• Peel the Jerusalem artichokes and the potato. Cut into pieces and place in a pan with the onion and chicken stock. Bring to a boil, then cover and simmer for 30 minutes.

• Meanwhile, trim off the mushroom stems and wipe the caps with damp paper towels. Cut the mushroom caps into 1/4-inch-thick slices.

• Heat the clarified butter in a sauté pan and add the mushroom slices, garlic halves, and lemon juice. Cook very gently until tender, browned, and almost caramelized. Season at the end of cooking.

• When the soup is cooked, purée in the pan with a hand-held immersion blender, or in a blender or food processor. Reheat if necessary. Stir in the cream and taste for seasoning.

• Pour into soup bowls and garnish with the caramelized mushrooms and parsley.

Serves 4-6
Preparation: 30 minutes
Cooking time: 35 minutes

1 lb Jerusalem artichokes (the less knobby the better, for easier peeling)

1 new potato

1 onion, sliced

4 cups chicken stock

12 shiitake mushrooms

1/4 cup clarified butter or olive oil

1 garlic clove, halved

2 teaspoons lemon juice

1/2 cup whipping cream

1 small bunch of fresh flat-leaf parsley, minced

salt and freshly ground white pepper

Shaker herb soup

• Peel the potatoes, then cut into quarters. Peel and slice the onions. Put the potatoes and onions in a large pan with enough cold water to cover. Salt lightly and cook over low heat, covered, for 25 minutes. Drain, reserving the cooking liquid. Purée the potatoes and onions with a food mill or in a blender.

• Heat two-thirds of the milk to boiling, then set aside. Heat the clarified butter in another large saucepan. Add half the parsley, the thyme, marjoram, and the savory and nettles if using. Add the flour and stir well, then add the remaining cold milk, the sugar, and seasoning to taste.

• Add the hot milk and stir until the soup begins to thicken. Stir in the potato purée, with some of the reserved potato cooking liquid if necessary to thin slightly. Taste for seasoning and heat through.

• Just before serving, stir in the butter, the remaining parsley, and the chives.

Serves 6
Preparation: 40 minutes
Cooking time:
about 30 minutes

6 new potatoes
2 onions
3 cups milk
2 tablespoon clarified butter
6 tablespoons minced fresh flat-leaf parsley
2 teaspoons minced fresh thyme leaves
2 teaspoons minced fresh marjoram
1 teaspoon minced savory (optional)
6 sprigs of small, fresh, young nettles, minced (optional, but wear gloves)
2 tablespoons flour
1 teaspoon sugar
2 tablespoons unsalted butter
3 tablespoons snipped fresh chives
salt and freshly ground white pepper

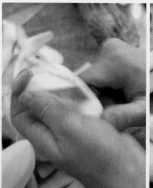

Pumpkin soup with buttery leeks

Serves 4
Preparation:
40 minutes
Cooking time:
about 30 minutes

1 small pumpkin, about
1½ lb

4 cups chicken stock

2 leeks

¼ cup clarified butter

a few shavings of Cheddar
or Cantal cheese (optional)

fresh chives, snipped with
scissors

salt and freshly ground
white pepper

• Cut the pumpkin into largish pieces, then peel and remove seeds. Cut the peeled pieces into cubes and put in a saucepan. Add the stock (or water) and bring to a boil, then cover and simmer gently for 30 minutes. Drain, reserving the stock. Purée the pumpkin in a blender or with a food mill. Stir into the stock. If the soup is too thick, add some water. Taste for seasoning and set aside.

• Wash and trim the leeks, leaving 4 inches of the green part. Slice, but not too thinly. Heat the butter in a pan over medium heat. Add the leek slices and cook until golden, then lower the heat and cook for a few more minutes. They should be just browned and lightly caramelized.

• Reheat the pumpkin soup, adding the leeks at the last minute.

• To serve, ladle into serving bowls, add a few cheese shavings to each, if desired, and sprinkle with chives.

Serves 6-8
Preparation: 30 minutes
Cooking time: about 2 hours
Soaking time: 6 hours

¼ cup dried chickpeas (garbanzo beans) (or use 2 cups shelled fresh green peas) • 1 large pinch of baking soda • 1½ lb boneless lamb neck slices • ½ cup pearl barley • 1 carrot, finely diced • 1 celery stalk, finely diced • 1 turnip, finely diced • 1 large onion, minced • 1 fresh bouquet garni (parsley, bay leaf, and thyme or savory) • 2 large leeks, with a bit of green • 8 sprigs of fresh flat-leaf parsley • 3 sprigs of fresh mint • 4 tablespoons unsalted butter • 1 lemon, quartered • salt, coarsely ground pepper, and freshly ground pepper

Scotch broth

• If using chickpeas, soak for 6 hours in enough cold water to cover, with the baking soda added.

• Bring 6 cups of water to a boil in a large saucepan. Salt lightly and add the lamb. Return to a boil, skimming the surface frequently to remove any foam, then add the drained chickpeas and the pearl barley. Stir well.

• When the liquid returns to a boil, add the carrot, celery, turnip, onion, bouquet garni, and coarse pepper. Lower the heat, cover, and simmer gently until the meat is tender, about 1½ hours. Remove the lamb with a slotted spoon. If using fresh peas, add them at this point and continue to simmer.

• Meanwhile, cut the meat into small pieces. Return to the soup. Taste and adjust the seasoning, then simmer for 10 more minutes.

• Cut the white of leeks into ½-inch-thick slices, and mince the green part. Mince the parsley and mint. Add the white leek slices to the soup and simmer gently for 5 minutes. Remove from the heat and stir in the minced leek greens, parsley, and mint, and the butter. Stir well.

• Serve with some crusty bread and lemon quarters for squeezing, as desired.

Creamy Hungarian beet soup with caraway seeds

• Peel and mince the onion. Cut the beets into fine dice. Heat the goose or duck fat, or oil, in a large saucepan over medium heat, add the onion and caraway seeds, and cook, stirring constantly, for 5 minutes. When the onion is soft but not browned, add the teaspoon of paprika and cook, stirring, for a few seconds; do not burn. Add the beets and stir, then add the beef stock. Bring to a simmer and cook over low heat for 10 minutes.

• Meanwhile, combine the flour and crème fraîche in a bowl. Stir well and add the vinegar to thin. Add water, if necessary, to thin further. Set aside.

• Purée the beet soup in a blender or with a food mill. Return to the heat and stir in the crème fraîche mixture. Bring gently to simmering point, stirring, and cook for 1 minute over low heat.

• Serve hot, garnished with chives, crème fraîche, chopped walnuts, and paprika.

Serves 6
Preparation: 25 minutes
Cooking time: 15 minutes

1 small onion
4 cooked beets, peeled
1 tablespoon goose or duck fat or olive oil
$^1/_2$ teaspoon caraway seeds
1 teaspoon Hungarian paprika
4 cups beef stock
1 tablespoon flour
4 tablespoons crème fraîche
3–4 tablespoons vinegar

• **For the garnish:**
fresh chives snipped with scissors, crème fraîche, chopped walnuts, Hungarian paprika

Belgian onion soup with ale

• Peel and thinly slice the onions. Heat the butter in a large saucepan, add the onions, and cook gently until soft. Add the stock and beer, and season. Simmer gently for 30 minutes. Taste for seasoning.

• Preheat the broiler. Put the slices of bread on a baking sheet and toast on both sides under the broiler. Cover with the grated cheese and broil until the cheese is melted and lightly browned.

• Ladle the soup into bowls and top each with a slice of toasted bread. Serve immediately.

Serves 4
Preparation: 30 minutes
Cooking time: 30 minutes

2 large, red onions
6 tablespoons clarified butter
2 cups chicken or beef stock
3 cups strong Belgian beer (bière de garde) or strong ale
4 thick slices of rustic bread
6 heaped tablespoons grated Parmesan cheese (or use Gruyère)
salt and freshly ground pepper

Helpful hints
for winter

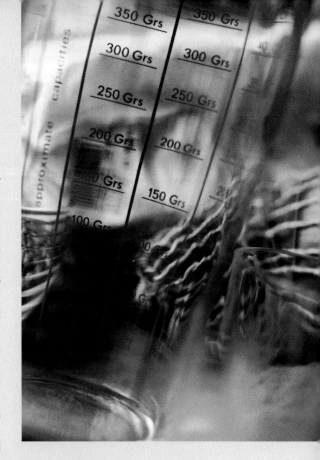

As soon as the first frost appears, it's time for robust soups based on legumes: dried beans, peas, and lentils. In order to get the best from these ingredients, be sure to allow adequate soaking and cooking time. Adding baking soda to the soaking water will help to shorten the soaking time (this works especially well for chickpeas). Rinse carefully and cook in fresh water. The outer skins of chickpeas can be removed by rubbing them between your fingers, after soaking. When cooking any kind of bean, use filtered water, or spring water with a low mineral content, as this will help to tenderize them; hard water should be avoided when cooking legumes. Finally, check any use-by date on packages. Fresher beans will give the best results—ideally, you should use beans within a year of being harvested. When cooking with stock, salt lightly, or not at all. Lemon juice can partially replace salt, so don't oversalt when using lemon juice in a soup. The important thing is to taste regularly during cooking.

• Stock made from poultry or meat can be refrigerated without degreasing, but do not leave it for more than 3 days before skimming off the fat. Concentrated stock cubes can also be made by reducing stocks as much as desired (do not over-season if reducing a great deal) and freezing in ice cube trays.

• **Chicken stock:** chicken carcass (raw or cooked, with giblets) or a whole chicken, bouquet garni, black peppercorns, small slice of ginger, a few vegetables (onion, celery, tomato, etc,—optional). Cover the chicken with water and bring to a boil, skimming any foam that rises to the surface, then lower the heat, add the remaining ingredients, salt lightly, and simmer gently, covered, for 2½ hours.

• **Beef or veal stock:** 2 lb meaty beef shanks, or veal shanks, bouquet garni, black peppercorns, small slice of ginger, onion, garlic, carrots, celery, etc. Prepare as for chicken stock, simmering gently, covered, for 3–4 hours.

Portuguese cabbage soup (caldo verde)

• Peel the potatoes. Peel and mince the onion and garlic. Heat some olive oil in a large saucepan, add the onion and garlic, and cook until soft and just browning. Add the potatoes and cook, stirring, for 2 minutes. Add 6 cups of water and bring to a boil, then lower the heat, cover, and simmer gently until the potatoes are tender, about 25 minutes.

Serves 6
Preparation: 30 minutes
Cooking time:
about 30 minutes

6 new potatoes
1 large onion
1 large garlic clove
olive oil
5 oz Spanish or Portuguese chorizo, sliced
1 lb Napa cabbage, Savoy cabbage, or turnip greens
salt and freshly ground black pepper

• Heat some olive oil in a frying pan, add the chorizo slices, and cook for a few minutes. Set aside. Wash the cabbage and drain well.

• Mash the potatoes thoroughly into the cooking liquid, or use a potato ricer. Add the chorizo slices, season with salt and pepper, and continue to cook over low heat.

• Meanwhile, roll up the cabbage leaves, a few at a time, and thinly slice across to obtain a julienne. Add to the soup and cook for a few more minutes until tender or al dente, according to your own taste.

• Serve with olive oil and sliced rustic bread.

Potato and leek soup, Normandy-style

• Wash the leeks thoroughly and trim, leaving about 3 inches of the green part. Slice the leek whites thinly; reserve the green part. Peel and dice the potatoes. Put the leek whites and potatoes into a large pan, add 4 cups of water, and bring to a boil. Salt lightly. Cover, lower the heat, and simmer gently for 30 minutes.

• Purée the soup in a food mill. Return to the pan and taste for seasoning.

• Thinly slice the green part of the leeks. Bring the soup to a gentle simmer, add the leek greens, cover, and remove from the heat. Let stand for 5 minutes.

• Ladle into bowls. Top each with a pat of butter or a dollop of cream and some ground pepper, and serve with crusty, fresh bread.

Serves 4-6
Preparation: 30 minutes
Cooking time:
30 minutes

4 large leeks
4 potatoes (about 1 lb)
unsalted butter or thick cream
salt and freshly ground pepper

Serves 4-6
Preparation: 1 hour
Cooking time: 1½ hours

1 cup toor dal (yellow split lentils) • ½ lime, scrubbed • 1 teaspoon ground turmeric • 1 large piece of dried tamarind • ¼ cup clarified butter • 4 teaspoons cumin seeds • 10 large garlic cloves • 1 large, ripe tomato • 2 tablespoons coriander seeds • ½ tablespoon black peppercorns • 1 dried, hot red chili pepper • 1 pinch of asafetida (available from Asian markets) • fresh cilantro leaves, shredded • salt • **For the garnish:** 2 garlic cloves, sliced • 8 curry leaves • 1 teaspoon black mustard seeds • ½ teaspoon cumin seeds • 2 tablespoons white mustard seeds

Lentil soup with garlic and tomato (rasam)

• Rinse the lentils thoroughly. Put them in a large pot with enough water to cover them by about 1 inch. Add the lime half and turmeric, and bring to a boil. Cook until the lentils are tender, about 1 hour. Drain, reserving the cooking liquid. Discard the lime half. Crush the lentils, then stir them into the reserved liquid.

• Soak the tamarind in hot water for 5 minutes, then press through a fine sieve to extract the pulp.

• Heat some of the clarified butter. Add 1 teaspoon of the cumin seeds and the whole peeled garlic cloves, and cook until just golden. Peel, seed, and mince the tomato. Add to the garlic and cumin mixture, and purée in a blender.

• With a spice mill, grind together the coriander seeds, peppercorns, remaining cumin seeds, and the chili pepper. In a pan, combine the ground spices with the tamarind pulp, asafetida, and some salt. Bring to a boil. Stir in the tomato mixture, then the lentils and their liquid. Thin with water if necessary. Taste for seasoning and simmer gently for 30 minutes.

• For the garnish: Heat the remaining clarified butter, add all of the garnish ingredients, and cook until golden. Bring the soup back to a boil and stir in the garnish mixture, then remove from the heat and let stand for 3 minutes.

• Serve hot, sprinkled with shredded cilantro leaves.

Cock-a-leekie (Scottish chicken soup)

Serves 6
Preparation: 30 minutes
Cooking time: about 2 hours

8 cups chicken stock (or water) • 8 large leeks • 1 small free-range chicken, about 2 lb • 10 black peppercorns • 8 allspice berries • 2 whole cloves • 1 pinch of ground mace • 3 sprigs of fresh flat-leaf parsley • 12 plump prunes with pits

• Bring the stock (or water) to a boil. Meanwhile, wash the leeks thoroughly and trim, leaving 2 inches of the green part. Slice 3 of the leeks finely. When the stock comes to a boil, add the chicken and the sliced leeks. Wrap all the spices and the parsley in a small square of cheesecloth and tie securely. Add the spice bundle to the cooking chicken. Cover, lower the heat, and simmer gently for 1½ hours. Degrease by blotting the surface with paper towels.

• Cut the remaining leeks into 1-inch rounds; mince a bit of the green part and put to one side for the garnish.

• Add the prunes to the soup. Bring back to a simmer and continue cooking for 20 minutes. Remove from the heat. Lift out the chicken and cut into serving pieces; keep hot. Add the rounds of leek to the soup and let stand, covered, for 3 minutes.

• Serve the chicken pieces alongside the soup, on a separate platter, or put some sliced chicken into each serving bowl and ladle in the soup, making sure everyone has leek pieces and a couple of prunes. Garnish the soup with a sprinkling of minced leek greens.

Serves 6-8
Preparation: 30 minutes
Cooking time: 30 minutes

1 large carrot • 1 celery stalk • 1 large onion • 3 cups beer
(lager or ale) • 2 tablespoons chicken bouillon powder
• 2 tablespoons flour • 3 cups milk • 1 lb aged Cheddar
cheese, shredded or crumbled (about 4 cups) • salt and
freshly ground pepper

American Cheddar
and beer soup

• Peel the carrot and cut into fine match-sticks (julienne). Cut the celery into fine dice. Peel and mince the onion.

• Combine the beer and chicken bouillon powder in a large saucepan. Bring slowly to a boil, stirring occasionally, then add the carrot, celery, and onion. Cover and simmer gently for 10 minutes

• In a small bowl, mix the flour with one-third of the milk, adding the milk little by little. Gradually pour this mixture into the hot soup, whisking until it is completely incorporated.

• Add the remaining milk and return to a boil. Lower the heat and cook until the soup begins to thicken slightly, about 15 minutes, stirring frequently. Gradually add the cheese, stirring well between each addition to melt thoroughly. Season generously and cook very gently for 1 more minute.

• Serve immediately, with slices of crusty baguette.

African fish gombo

• Salt the fish fillets and cut into large pieces. Sprinkle the eel slices with lime juice. Set all the fish aside. Rinse the okra, trim the stem end, and slice thinly into rounds.

• Place the stock in a large pan and add one chili-pepper quarter, the okra, tomatoes, and baking soda. Bring to a boil, then reduce the heat and simmer gently for 10–15 minutes. Chop the spinach coarsely and add to the soup, along with the eel and some salt. Cover and simmer gently for 20 minutes. Meanwhile, remove the skin and bones from the smoked mackerel and flake the flesh into large pieces.

• Taste the soup for seasoning. Add the pieces of white fish, the smoked mackerel, and the remaining chili pepper quarters. Simmer gently for 3–5 minutes. Remove from the heat and add the red palm oil, stirring gently to incorporate.

• Serve with rice or cornmeal mush.

Serves 6
Preparation: 1 hour
Cooking time: 35 minutes

1 lb white fish fillets (haddock, halibut, cod, sole, etc.)
10 oz eel slices
juice of ½ lime
1 lb okra
2 cups fresh, strong fish or beef stock
1 Scotch bonnet or habanero chili pepper, seeded and quartered
14 oz canned crushed tomatoes
pinch of baking soda
8 oz fresh spinach, washed and trimmed
1 whole smoked mackerel
1 cup red palm oil (zomi, available from African markets)
salt and freshly ground pepper
cooked white rice or cornmeal mush, for serving

Italian consommé (beef bouillon with egg and Parmesan)

• Preheat the oven to 350°F. Heat the butter in a frying pan, add the bread slices, and cook until golden brown on both sides. Put one slice in each serving bowl and put them into the oven to keep warm.

Serves 6
Preparation: 30 minutes
Cooking time:
10 minutes

¹/₄ **cup clarified butter**

6 slices of rustic sourdough bread, such as Poilâne

6 cups strong beef or chicken stock

6 fresh eggs

6 heaped tablespoons freshly grated Parmesan cheese

minced fresh flat-leaf parsley

freshly grated nutmeg

salt and freshly ground pepper

• Bring the stock to a boil, and taste for seasoning.

• Remove the bowls from the oven. Break an egg onto each slice of bread, then ladle the boiling stock over. Season with pepper. Let stand for 3 minutes to allow the egg white to set, then sprinkle generously with Parmesan, minced parsley, and grated nutmeg. Serve immediately.

Hungarian goulash soup

• Cut the beef into 1-inch cubes. Peel the onions and chop coarsely. Heat the lard or butter in a Dutch oven, add the onions, and cook until soft and translucent, about 10 minutes. Add the beef and cook for 10 more minutes over medium heat.

• Crush the garlic with the caraway seeds and some salt. Remove the pot from the heat and stir in the garlic paste and the paprika, mixing well. Add 8 cups of water, then cover and simmer gently for 1 hour.

• Peel, seed, and chop the tomato. Core and slice the bell pepper. Add both to the soup, with more water if necessary. Simmer for a further 30 minutes.

• Peel the potatoes and cut into large cubes. Add to the soup and cook until tender, about 20 more minutes. Taste for seasoning.

• Serve in deep soup bowls, with crusty bread and a good red wine.

Serves 6
Preparation: 30 minutes
Cooking time: just over 2 hours

2 lb chuck steak
2 large onions
2 tablespoons lard or clarified butter
1 garlic clove
pinch of caraway seeds
3 tablespoons mild Hungarian paprika (or use 2 tablespoons mild and 1 tablespoon hot)
1 large, ripe tomato
1 red or green bell pepper
1 lb new potatoes
salt

Peking sweet-sour soup

Serves 6
Preparation: 50 minutes
Cooking time: 12–15 minutes

36 dried lily buds (available from Asian markets)
6 large, dried Chinese mushrooms
1 handful of dried Chinese mushrooms, such as tree ears
1 boneless chicken breast half
1 egg
toasted sesame and peanut oils
¼-inch-thick slice of fresh ginger, chopped
1 tablespoon soy sauce
2 tablespoons Chinese rice wine
4 cups chicken stock
2 tablespoons cornstarch mixed with ¼ cup water
1 piece of firm tofu, cubed
¾ cup chopped peeled raw shrimp
1 green onion, chopped
salt

• For the marinade:
1 tablespoon soy sauce
1 tablespoon Chinese rice wine
1 teaspoon sugar
1 teaspoon cornstarch
1 tablespoon toasted sesame oil

• For the sweet-sour sauce:
2 tablespoons red wine vinegar
1 tablespoon soy sauce
1 teaspoon ground white pepper
2 teaspoons Chinese chili oil
1 tablespoon toasted sesame oil

• Make the marinade and the sweet-sour sauce by combining the ingredients in two small bowls. Set aside.

• Put the lily buds and mushrooms in separate bowls and add hot water to cover. Soak for 30 minutes to soften. Drain and clean them, trimming the hard tips of the lily buds. Slice the mushrooms. Cut the chicken into thin slices, then toss in the marinade and set aside. Beat the egg with a little sesame oil.

• Heat some peanut oil in a wok over high heat. Add the ginger and chicken, season, and stir-fry for 1 minute. Remove the chicken, and add the mushrooms and lily buds. Stir-fry for 1 minute, then add the soy sauce, wine, and stock. Bring to a boil, then lower the heat and simmer for 10 minutes.

• Raise the heat, add the cornstarch mixture, and cook until the soup thickens. Remove from the heat and gently stir in the beaten egg. Add the tofu, chicken, and shrimp.

• Pour half of the sweet-sour sauce into a tureen, fill with the soup, and top with the remaining sauce. Garnish with the chopped green onion and serve.

Serves 6
Preparation: 30 minutes
Cooking time: 2¾ hours

2 cups dried black beans • pinch of baking soda • pinch of ground cumin • 2 pinches of dried oregano • 1 bay leaf • 4 bottled jalapeño peppers, seeded if desired • 4 ripe tomatoes • 3 large garlic cloves • 3 onions • 1 large bunch of fresh cilantro • 1 celery stalk • 1 tablespoon red wine vinegar • 2 tablespoons olive oil • 4 tablespoons dry sherry • salt and freshly ground pepper

Mexican black bean soup with salsa

• Rinse and pick over the beans. Place in a large pot, add plenty of cold water and the baking soda, and bring to a boil. Boil for 5 minutes, then add the cumin, oregano, and bay leaf. Cover and simmer gently for 1 hour.

• Mince 2 of the jalapeño peppers and add to the beans. Cook for a further 1–1½ hours or until the beans are tender, adding more water if necessary.

• Peel, seed, and mince the tomatoes. Peel and mince the garlic and onions. Mince the cilantro, celery, and remaining jalapeño peppers.

• For the salsa, combine half the tomatoes, one-third of the onions and garlic, all the minced cilantro and jalapeños, and the wine vinegar. Season liberally with salt and pepper. Cover and set aside.

• When the beans are tender, remove from the heat. Heat the olive oil in a pan, add the remaining onion and garlic, and cook for 5 minutes. Add the celery and the rest of the tomatoes, and cook for 10 minutes, to reduce.

• Purée half the bean soup, then stir in the tomato mixture. Stir this into the remaining bean soup, along with the sherry. Taste for seasoning.

• Serve hot, with a dollop of salsa in the middle of each bowl, accompanied by fresh bread.

Columbian chicken soup (ajiaco)

• Peel and slice the onions. Peel all the potatoes. Cut the large potatoes into thin slices and set aside. Put the baby potatoes in cold water and set aside.

• In a large, heavy pot, heat the butter or oil. Add the chicken pieces and onions, and cook until golden. Add the potato slices and stock. Bring to a boil, then lower the heat and simmer gently for 25 minutes. Add the baby potatoes and cook for 20 more minutes.

• Remove the chicken pieces and the baby potatoes from the soup. Purée the soup in a blender, or with a food mill, and return to the pot. Taste for seasoning, then return the chicken and baby potatoes to the soup. Add the corn kernels and the capers. Simmer for 5 minutes. Just before serving, stir in the whipping cream.

• For the sauce, crush the avocado flesh and mix with the chopped egg yolk. Add the remaining sauce ingredients and mix well.

• Serve the soup with the avocado sauce on the side.

Serves 4
Preparation: 40 minutes
Cooking time:
about 1 hour

2 large onions
1 lb baby new potatoes
4 large red or new potatoes
1/4 cup clarified butter or olive oil
1 free-range chicken, about
2 1/2 lb, cut into 8 pieces,
(or use 2 lb chicken thighs,
cut into pieces)
8 cups chicken stock
3 cups canned corn kernels,
yellow or white, undrained
3 tablespoons capers
1/2 cup whipping cream
salt and freshly ground pepper

• **For the avocado sauce:**
1 large, ripe Haas avocado
1 hard-cooked egg, white and
yolk chopped separately
1 green onion, minced
2 tablespoons minced fresh
cilantro
1/4 Habanero chili pepper, minced,
or more to taste
1 tablespoon white wine vinegar
salt and pepper

Mexican meatball soup

• Peel, seed, and chop the tomato. Peel and mince the onion. Heat some olive oil in a pan, add the onion, and cook over medium heat until golden. Add the tomato, jalapeño, sugar, and a pinch each of salt and pepper. Cook until thick.

• Soak the bread crumbs in milk for a few seconds, then squeeze dry. Mix with the veal, raisins, a pinch of grated nutmeg, the Parmesan, and the warm tomato sauce. Add the eggs and mix thoroughly . Shape into balls about 2 inches in diameter and set aside.

• To prepare the broth: Cook the onion in a little olive oil until soft, then add the stock, wine, and herbs, and boil for a few minutes. Season with salt and pepper, then carefully add the meatballs. Cover and simmer gently for 40 minutes. Add more stock or wine if the liquid reduces too much.

• Serve in soup bowls, garnished with chopped cilantro.

Serves 4
Preparation: 1 hour
Cooking time:
40–50 minutes

• For the meatballs:
1 ripe tomato
1 onion
olive oil
1 bottled jalapeño pepper, minced
1 teaspoon sugar
1 cup fine, fresh bread crumbs
a little milk
1 lb ground veal
6 tablespoons golden raisins
¼ cup freshly grated Parmesan cheese
2 eggs
chopped fresh cilantro
salt, freshly ground pepper, and grated nutmeg

• For the broth:
1 onion, minced
3 cups beef stock
1¼ cups good red wine
1 large pinch of dried thyme
1 large pinch of dried oregano
1 bay leaf

Scottish smoked haddock soup

• Peel and mince the onion. Heat the clarified butter in a pan, add the onion, and cook over low heat until soft, about 5 minutes. Cut the haddock into large pieces, keeping the skin on, and add to the onion. Add enough water just to cover and bring to a boil. Cover and simmer gently for 8 minutes. Meanwhile, peel the potatoes, cut into large pieces, and boil or steam until cooked.

• Remove the fish from the soup and set aside to cool. Reserve the cooking liquid. Mash the potatoes finely with a potato ricer until smooth. Remove the bones and skin from the haddock, then flake the flesh finely.

• Gradually stir the haddock cooking liquid into the mashed potatoes, then stir in the milk, followed by the haddock pieces. If the soup is too thick, add a little water. Bring to a boil, then lower the heat and simmer gently for 10 minutes. Add a generous grinding of pepper and stir in the parsley. Let stand for 3 minutes.

• Serve hot, with a pat of butter or a dollop of crème fraîche in each bowl, sprinkled with snipped chives.

Serves 4
Preparation: 25 minutes
Cooking time: 18 minutes

1 onion
¼ cup clarified butter
1 smoked haddock fillet (finnan haddie), about 1 lb
2 large new potatoes, about 12 oz
2 cups milk (or use 1 cup whipping cream and 1 cup water)
chopped fresh flat-leaf parsley and chives
freshly ground pepper
unsalted butter or crème fraîche, for serving

index of recipes

Italian consommé (beef bouillon with egg and Parmesan) 80

Ivory Coast avocado soup 48

Jelled beet consommé 12

Lentil soup with garlic and tomato (rasam) 75

Mango and melon soup 46

Mexican black bean soup with salsa 86

Mexican meatball soup 90

Normandy apple and potato soup 26

Peking sweet-sour soup 85

Portuguese cabbage soup (caldo verde) 70

Potato and leek soup, Normandy-style 72

Provençal vegetable soup (soupe au pistou) 18

Pumpkin soup with buttery leeks 61

Scotch broth 62

Scottish smoked haddock soup 92

Senegalese shrimp soup with coconut 39

Shaker herb soup 58

Strawberry soup with balsamic vinegar 22

Vichyssoise with watercress 14